ISBN 978-0-259-48903-0
PIBN 10819504

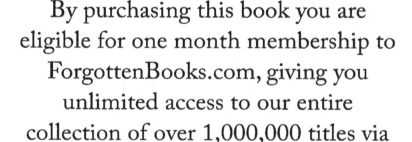

MELCHIZEDEK

OR

The Secret Doctrine of the Bible

BY

J. C. F. GRUMBINE

Published by
The Order of the White Rose, B.B.P.O.
Boston, Mass.

COPYRIGHTED, 1919

MATTHEW 13:35

"I **WILL** UTTER THINGS WHICH
HAVE BEEN KEPT SECRET
FROM THE FOUNDATION
OF THE WORLD"

CONTENTS

INTRODUCTION

The Bible has been regarded as a sealed book, its mysteries impenetrable, its knowledge unfathomable, its key lost. Even its miracles have been so excluded from scientific research as to be invested with a supernaturalism which forever separated them from the possibility of human understanding and rational interpretation.

In the midst of these revolutionary times, it is not strange that theology and institutional Christianity should feel the foundations of their authority slipping from them, and a new, broader and more spiritual thought of man and

God taking their places. All this is a part of the general awakening of mankind and has not come about in a day or a year. It grew. It is still growing, because the soul is eternal and justifies and vindicates its own unfoldment.

Some see in this new birth of man the annihilation of church and state, but others who are more informed and illumined, realize that the chaff and dross of error are being separated from the wheat and gold of truth and that only the best, and that which is for the highest good of mankind will remain.

It is a pity that the church must continually perish that the truth shall shine in perfect and eternal splendor. Would that the church could let the light of Divine Truth so shine that creeds, theologies and ritual might be revised to meet the present and progressive needs of the human soul.

Religion does not depend for its existence upon the church, but the church depends upon religion.

The moral and spiritual teachings of the Bible are revelations only in so far as they agree with truth, and truth alone determines the spiritual substance of revelation.

The church will not wholly pass away. What will and must die in all ecclesiastical institutions is that which limits man's freedom to know the truth.

The Bible, no less than other books

on religion and science must stand the tests of time. Its supreme importance to man is not its literature or history but its revelation. All revelation is from within the soul. It is mixed and fused with extraneous and alien matter. It opens one page while it closes another. No Simon pure revelation of truth has ever been given to the world. It must touch the sphere of human intelligence to be perceived and received, and through the purest channel it is tinctured by personality. It must be adapted to the needs of the generations to which it is sent. It is presented in symbols, allegories, parables and myths. Its doctrines are comparative as well as absolute. In the one, the letter killeth, in the other, the spirit giveth life. Jesus approved of and confirmed what is here said when he told his disciples that "the spirit of truth will lead you into all truth, until you shall know the truth and the truth shall make you free." But "what is truth?" asked Pilate and the question repeats itself to every honest soul. It is never simple, because it is many sided. Its facets are infinite. At best, we can speak of the truth about this or that doctrine of religion, philosophy and science, but the truth like mathematics is self contained and sustained, infinite and eternal.

Facts are appearances of the working of the law of natural and spiritual casuality. Religion and the church, in the universal sense, deal with these spiritual facts, which are their credentials and on which they build their technique and teaching of human and divine service. Without them, religion as well as the church would be without the "witness." The supreme purpose and aim of the "witness," is not to extract it out of all relationship with the other credentials and material facts of life, but to reveal the spirit of life, which has no other means at hand to prove its transcendent and independent reality, except to show that whereas the material phenomena of life appear to spring up from potential matter as a fact of life, both are traced back to and within Spirit. This is the supreme revelation of Jesus, when he affirmed, "I am the resurrection and the life."

The Bible as well as the soul reveal clearly four specific strata or spheres of human unfoldment. First, the historical, second the occult, third, the astro theological (the Law) and fourth, the mystical. The latter is demonstrated by the statements of Jesus. "I and the Father are one" and "I am in the Father and the Father is in me."

The first or historical is plain to everyone. The occult is that which is involved in mysteries, such as "the hidden wisdom", concealed in parables, myths, symbols, allegories, dreams, visions, prophesies, signs, miracles, the gnosis, lost word, canon, cabala, with which the Bible abounds, but which must be penetrated before the object of the Bible as a revelation is understood. This, the "thus saith the Lord," or the working of the Law as typified by the astro theological sphere makes clear. "God geometrizes," wrote Ralph Waldo Emerson, and Pythagoras, an ancient Greek philosopher, had inscribed on the portal of his temple, "Let no one enter here who is ignorant of geometry." "There is," said the author of Proverbs, "a time and a place for everything under the sun," and Jesus emphasized the same truth when he added "every hair of your head is numbered." This, briefly, signifies that Law governs life and that that Law is of spirit, that "action and reaction are equal, that whatsoever a man sows, that will he also reap," and that underneath the operations of natural phenomena (effects and results) is the Law of the Spirit, revealing its absolute and eternal Majesty and Sovereignty in each form of cell, corpuscle and organism.

History manifests what the Law occultly reveals.

The object of this book is to hint and reveal, so far as it is practical, the Secret Doctrine of the Bible, that we may no longer grope in darkness or blindness and that the seamless robe of Christ may be our inheritance.

LECTURE 1

Who is Melchizedek? Biblical History. His Office and His Order.

All that is known historically of Melchizedek is contained in the Bible, in Genesis 4: 18; Psalms 110 and Hebrews 5: 6, 7. The incident which connects him with history is the story of how Abraham, returning to his own country with the spoils captured from Chedorlaomer who was battling Lot, his sons and tribe and whom Abraham sought to rescue, gave tithes to this superior functionary, Melchizedek, high priest of righteousness and king of Salem, city of peace. It relates how

14

this distinguished priest of the most high God refreshed Abraham with bread and wine and bestowed upon him his blessing, making him a priest of his own order.

Who Melchizedek was is not made clear. Numerous speculations arise as to his identity. He is said to be without birth and death, father, mother and descent. As such, his existence is involved in mystery. He is invested with fanciful and mythological conceits. Some, however, trace him back to a father of one branch of the human race, to Shem and others to Noah. The astro mythological connection is even more obscure. He is regarded by certain authorities (Bryant in Analysis of Ancient Mythology) as Sadik or Sy (Zedek), who is also identified with Cronus (Father Time) or Saturn, personifications of planetary principles or gods. In fact, such personifications were not the exception, when the mystery of the relationship, between heavenly principles or astrological names and early historical characters as Cain, Abel; Noah, Abraham, Moses, are considered. For instance, Ab-Ram or Ab-Ra (h)am could easily be translated in the two derivatives—Ab and R. A. M. or A-Bram, meaning "from Right, Ascension, Meridian," Ab referring to father as Abba is father—and Bram or Bra(h)ma meaning God, the name of the Hindu deity in the trinity of which Siva and

Visnu are the other two, Brahma being
the God above every other God, the Absolute, Eternal, Unchanging One. Gerald Massey in "The Book of Begin-
nings," "Natural Genesis," and
"Egypt, the Light of the World," elab-
orates the source and connection of
Egyptian Mythology and ritualistic
mysteries with Christolatry, so that
Biblical history and New Testament
facts can be threshed from the mass of
the fictitious, apocryphal, symbological
literature which the Bible contains,
clearing the way for an ideal, metaphysical and spiritual interpretation of
such assumed historical persons as
Melchizedek.

Thus, when Melchizedek is likened

to the head of the human race, an angel, the son of God in human form, the Messiah, the potential representative on earth of the Christ and finally, the Holy Ghost, the student of the Secret Doctrine must not be swept off his feet by these claims, but must diligently and patiently inquire how and why such claims have been made, and why the name Melchizedek has lain like gold in the river bed of Biblical literature over which the river of life itself has long since ceased to flow.

It is true that historical persons have frequently been first canonized and then deified, as it is also true that mythological personifications of natural forces, laws and phenomena have been reduced to human beings. Osirus and Isis, once Egyptian prince and princess, some thousands of years ago, became in due course of time king and queen, and after the lapse of ages, a sun God and a moon God that were actually worshipped in temples dedicated to them. A similar metamorphic change and a deification of this sort is expected to be made of the late Mary Baker Eddy, founder of the Christian Science Church. A secret enmity has already arisen among the Roman Catholics against Christian Scientists because they see modern tendencies in that direction and fear that the throne of the Christian, Divine motherhood now occupied by Mary may be usurped by what may be called, in the terms of the shop, a spiritual competitor. All this sounds strange and uncanny to ears unaccustomed to the wild and audacious claims of supernaturalists, and Christian Science metaphysicians, but history often repeats itself.

Thus the language which invests Melchizedek with historical authenticity disguises his real self or Divinity. It can be said, with much assurance of certainty that Melchizedek symbolically and mystically typifies the personification as well as impersonation of the Holy Ghost which, in Genesis for the first time was mentioned in human history and made the representative emblem of man's divine heredity and Providence. Thus the Order was formed in the Spiritual Spheres, in the mystical sense and transferred to the sublime consciousness of a man, who was the alleged first enlightened God father of the Jews, Abraham. From him sprung the prophetic capacity, which is most virile and active among those who are of the Order of Melchizedek.

The sense of exalted, dignified, exclusiveness, separateness, and august divinity which clothed tha personality of the ancient Jewish prophets, was founded upon spiritual relationship which connected Abraham mystically with Melchizedek. Worthiness of body and mind, heroic and true in their consecration to truth, they became the high priests after the Order of Melchizedek, through whom was preserved the spirit of the original human vision and spiritual ideal of divine perfection, which in process of time, when the old school of major and minor prophets had closed their books of prophecy, the human realization and divine incarnation should come among mankind as the Messiah or Christ.

It was not improbable that this divine perfection should lodge potentially and inactively in the soul of man, until kindled into a conscious vision by a divine visitation as that of an angel, an avatar, an epiphany, and then enter upon its earthly travail in the womb of woman and the mind of man to celebrate its nativity, first in prophetic vision and afterward when cosmic and earthly conditions are ripe, to manifest in its perfect human incarnation. All this is hinted at in Genesis in the mysterious meeting of Melchizedek and Abraham.

LECTURE II

The Secret Doctrines of the Order. Its Myths, Mysteries, Symbolisms, Canons, Philosophy.

It is a well known fact that there was and still is a "Secret Doctrine" known to the ancient and ignored by the modern world, although glimpsed by certain God conscious and illumined souls as prophets or seers, and great racial teachers, and that this doctrine was hinted at by Paul in his references in the Hebrews to the Order Melchizedek. In a unique book printed in London 1897 and entitled, "The Canon," with an introduction by R. B. C. Graham, much is written about the pagan mystery perpetuated in the Cabala as the rule of all the arts. The supernal Adam (of the spirit or heavenly world) became the earthly Adam, since "the earth" to quote the Canon, "was philosophically considered to be the mother or receptive power in the planetary system, she was figuratively said to have conceived and brought forth the primeval man, the earth born Adam, the son of the supernal Adam. Thus, according to the Hebrews, the race of mortals was produced; and the spirit of life having been implanted in the body of the first man he transmitted it through Eve to all subsequent generations." This sounds vague, indefinite, unscientific, as it is to an evolutionist who does not accept as simple and allegorical an explanation of the origin of life or man on this planet. Such a solution, however, is by the traditionalists, animists, cabalists and advocates of the Secret Doctrine treated as a myth, not as an historical fact, the secret of human origin and birth, being withheld from and concealed in the parabolical language. Nor has modern science so far furnished the key, either to unlock the mystery or to explain the myth.

The word "involution" will help the student to understand the natural progress known as evolution, the ascending arc of life, which word involution psychical investigators are now throwing light upon as clearing up the false claims, first, of theologians as to a supernatural human origin, rather than a supernormal or divine, and secondly, of physical scientists who deny that man is a human soul and his origin or heredity is from God; thus by the denial, outlawing all other and spiritual evidences, which is included in and affirmed and confirmed by the spiritual hypothesis.

Bergson in "Matter and Memory" boldly claims that spirit has an existence of its own, "that there is in matter something more than, but something different from, that which is actually given. The truth is that there is one and only one, method of refuting materialism, it is to show that matter is precisely that which it appears to be. Thereby, we eliminate all virtuality, all hidden power, from matter and establish the phenomena of spirit as an independent reality. But to do this, we must leave to matter those qualities which materialists and spiritualists alike strip from it; the latter that they may make of them representations of the spirit, the former that they may regard them only as the accidental garb of space."

Thus Bergson defends the soul or spirit as an entity quite apart from matter and the material world, with which it is associated.

However, in the mysterious language

of Plato, the soul in its natural pilgrimage through life, exists in three distinct forms under diverse conditions. The human germ first exists in the body of man, who is the father. In the act of coition, it is transferred to the woman who is the mother, and in the third form, it is born into the world an independent human body, and as man or woman, it so remains until death. The first residence of the psychic germ is referred to in Hebrews 7: 9-10 "Levi also, who received tithes, payed tithes in Abraham. For he was yet in the loins of his father when Melchizedek met him." The transition from the first residence to the second marks the soul's first death and birth. This is symbolized by the Phoenix, rising again after distintegration and dissolution. The Phoenix was a sacred Egyptian and Greek mythological bird like an eagle, fabled as coming out of Arabia every five hundred years to Heliopolis, Egypt, the city of the sun, where it burnt itself on the altar and rose again from its ashes, young and beautiful. It became a perpetual type of immortality and the resurrection. Of course, the bird and the story is a myth, containing the ancient secret doctrine of the immortality of soul as manifest in human existence, growth and evolution.

The second stage of the soul's existence, is when it reaches as a germ the womb of the woman, the abode of darkness (sheol or hades of the Jews and Greeks), and in the third stage, as it issues from the womb, it has a substantial physical body and so begins its life as a man.

In this body, the soul was by the ancient teachers conceived as a spark of the divine essence of God, and so, thus endowed with Divinity, was capable of transmitting a portion of the soul within him, and being essentially immortal, added a "new link in the continuous chain of life, whose beginning was in heaven"—Salem, the city of peace.

This, briefly was, what is known as the gnosis, or Secret Doctrine of the soul's birth, existence and destiny as taught in the Scriptures and imparted to initiates at the celebration of the mysteries. Origen wrote, "We hope, after the troubles and struggles which we suffer here, to reach the highest heavens, and receiving, agreeably to the teaching of Jesus, the fountains of water that spring up into eternal life and being,† filled with the rivers of knowledge, shall be united with those waters that are said to be above the heavens, and which praise His name. As many of us as praise Him shall not be carried about by the revolution of the heaven (reincarnation?) but shall ever be engaged in the contemplation of the invisible things."* This was the

---

† See John 4.
* Against Celsus, Book 6, Chapter 20.

meaning of the Egyptian, Jewish and Greek mysteries, tracing all souls back, thread by thread, from son to father, culminating in the earth born Adam, and finally in the upward swing of the arc, after the downward swing of the arc of the circle had been completed, they hoped and believed that when death came, they would ascend (by the seven spirits or angels—the planets) into the firmament to join the choir of the stars, whence they issued.

The fall of man we know can now be satisfactorily explained, not by the intent or accident of a theological fall or by a doctrine of total depravity, but by a mystical gnosis, scientifically and philosophically explained by the involution of the soul in matter, or by the four verities* of Buddha as applied to the soul's human descent, and ascent as typified in the creation and generation of souls in the first Adam, and by the teachings of Jesus. For it is mystically stated by Paul, "As in Adam all die, so in Christ shall all be made alive." The gnosis or Secret Doctrine is the same essentially in all ethnic religions, could we but cultivate the inner sense of the meanings of parables, symbols, myths and cabala.

The canon of this gnosis or Secret

---

* Buddha taught that existence is caused by desire. His first verity is "Pain exists." Second verity, "The cause of pain is desire or attachment." Third verity, "Pain can be ended by Nirvana." Fourth verity, "The way is shown to Nirvana."

Doctrine was given by word of mouth by master builders and teachers called priests from temples in which they officiated, to the initiated, who according to the customs of the times concealed the teachings and the mysteries often in contradictory, grotesque and foolish symbolisms, for which the wise only held the key. Again, the gnosis was hidden away in the architectural plans of certain monuments as the pyramid and sphinx and in temples and cathedrals, as Solomon's temple and the cathedral of Milan. Homer wove it into his Iliad. Dante, incorporated it in his Divine Comedy, Milton in his story of Paradise Lost. Canonical theology and philosophy buried it in their sacred palimpsests. The epic story of the soul, is retold in the fourth chapter of John's Gospel, where Jesus addresses the woman of Samaria. **The**ology which was once **astro**logy, became such to conceal the Secret Doctrine from the worldly wise and prudent, for the same reason that alchemy became chemistry and astrology became astronomy, and so the Secret Doctrine was temporarily lost, at least, to those who preferred to receive orders from a Babel of confusion, rather than from the pillar of fire by night and the cloud of light by day.

LECTURE III

The Secret Doctrine on Four Planes of Expression and Manifestation.

In the metaphysical analysis of "Ehye Asher Ehyse", (I am that I am), the mystical source of the self consciousness, (ego or person) is contrasted with the consciousness of the Self, Divinity or God—the objective I or I objectified, with the subjective I or I subjectified. The former is conditioned by time, space and the necessity of experience, the latter is unconditioned, free. In the one, the ego is unaware and unconscious of its divinity, in the other it is quite aware and conscious of it.

In the Secret Doctrine of the Bible, it is taught that there are four elements and four principles, as well as four manifestations and expressions of life. The four elements are fire (oxygen), water (hydrogen), air (nitrogen) earth (carbon), necessary to organism or manifestation, and the four principles are divine or spiritual, psychic, mental and physical, necessary to expression.

Divinity or spirit, soul, mind, body constitute the four corner stones of life and have reference to the North, East, West and South, (NEWS), on which broadly speaking, the foundation of the Universe (Solomon's Temple) is built or established. This was implied in the plan of Solomon's temple, the outer court for the Gentiles (physical), the inner court for the Jews (mental), and the Holy of Holies for the high priest (psychic), where the fourth or Divine is realized. The physical, mental, psychic depend upon the Divine Being, thus completing the circle around the square of existence.

Fire among the alchemists and mystics has been symbolized by the sun, as water by the moon, the one masculine, (having the rose for its floral emblem) and the other feminine, (having the lily for its floral emblem). Fire is positive (magnetic) and water is electric or negative. Among the Hindus, fire is sacred to Siva and water to Vishnu, while the air (breath or spirit) would be sacred to Brahma, the third in the triune nature of the Hindu Godhead. As fire destroys outward form, Siva was called the destroyer, the father, and ruled over life and death, and as water preserves, Vishnu was called the preserver, and ruled over motherhood and children.

Fire has its metaphysical correpondent and symbolizes the active mind, the senses, the objective life, while water symbolizes the passive mind, the affections, the subjective life.

The sun germinates and generates life from seed by transforming the seed into its living potential form. Thus it is a destroyer. But the seed does not germinate until moistened by water.

And so the moon, ruling the water, the tides, woman, preserves the life in a form peculiar to its kind. Thus Siva and Vishnu, active and passive principles of deity (likened to light and darkness, heat and cold, evil and good) rule over spring and summer, autumn and winter respectively.

Manifestation is outer and physical (phenomenon), while expression is inner and mental, psychic and spiritual (neumonon). So that it can be said that the expression of the soul is to the sphere what the manifestation is to the plane of life. This must be kept continuously in mind if the student hopes to master the Secret Doctrine of the Bible. For how will he understand such mystical and occult sayings as this one of Hermes Tris Megistus, "As it is above, so is it below; as it is within, so it is without," and "whatever exists upon the earth in an earthly form, exists in the heavens in a heavenly form." And this profound saying of Iamblicus, "the day time of the body is the night time of the soul; the night time of the body is the day time of the soul." Spheres thus reflect their contents and substance on corresponding and kindred planes, according to the law of expression and manifestation. Gerald Massey thought that this correspondence is comprehended by the law of dissimilitude.

The soul, in fact, all life, essentially

spirit, functions on the four planes and in the four spheres, designated by the words, physical, mental, psychical and spiritual and is of one essence in all forms of expression and manifestation.

The soul or spirit does not create matter, but uses it. It vitalizes cells, attracts and arranges atoms, determines and disposes of the quality of the physical substance, and by its thought, feeling and character builds and destroys forms and transforms its body into the images (subjects and objects) it loves. Thus, the physical body and the human personality are related integrally to the psychic, spiritual and Divine Entity.*

----

* Entity is here employed to include one's Divinity.

It is a well known and established teaching in the Secret Doctrine of the Bible, that the ladder on which Jacob (the soul expressing itself) saw angels ascending and descending, is none other than the expression of the technique or Secret Doctrine applied to the soul's own powers or spiritual faculties, which, transcending the sphere and limitations of the senses and faculties of the natural man, afford a means of escape from time and space and the obsessions of the human brain to bask in the infinitude of eternity, where time is no more, and where the soul itself is free to live untrammeled by the flesh.

Abraham on the plains of Mamre realizes that the soul is never born and never dies. This followed his initiation into the Order of Melchizedek, who honored him by placing upon his shoulders the mantle of authority, the symbol of his illumined consciousness and so made him a high priest of spiritual revelation. Jacob, symbolizes the soul in the act of expressing as well as unfolding itself, while Isaac, is the symbol of all personal and physical sacrifices which each one must and will make, who aspires to be a high priest of the Order of Melchizedek, or, who, having obtained membership, is now serving at the altar of truth and helping others to do the same.

Now it is strange that the meaning of the word miracle should have been confused or mixed with the word supernatural, for the two words become meaningless in human psychology. What the soul cannot do and God can, make the soul's efforts seem helpless and hopeless. But when the soul's divinity is involved in God, both being of one essence, will, intelligence and life, the words miracle and supernatural become intelligible in the supreme, divine results which are attained by supreme divine efforts, the divinity of the soul expressing its divine attributes as omnipresence, omnipotence, omniscience and perfect love, attributes which are potential qualities of the soul and demonstrable on the four planes of expression. If supernaturalism suggests the idea of deus ex machina (a deity out-

side the machine), and the word miracle, an act of such a deity, then the
idea is unnatural and erroneous. If, on
the other hand, the soul can and does
express its divinity, so that it sees, hears
and feels beyond the power, law and
limitation of the senses, these results
are not to be accepted as supernatural,
however, they are to be classified as
supernormal (above the normal), and
are not miracles*, because they occur
under divine law. The Secret Doctrine
of the Bible assures us that the inner
sense of the Scripture depends upon the
use we make of our psychic and spir-

---

* A miracle is an act or result which takes place
by the suspension of natural law by the direct fiat of
God.

itual powers. And only the mystic who realizes that his divinity and its powers alone are a lamp to his feet and a light to his intelligence has a right to negotiate his powers and personality in this divine business. Does our coin bear the superscription of Caesar or of God?

If the Secret Doctrine of the Bible makes demands upon us and these demands when obeyed condition results, he would be foolish who expected to stand on the outer court of the temple, and hope to receive results which belong to those who have prepared themselves to be worthy of the Holy of Holies. Even such as are admitted to the inner court may see the vision clearer and hear the voice deeper, because of the degree of spiritual attainment, but they must prepare themselves for what is yet to come. Mere intellectuality, culture or refinement, however, or self love, egotism and ambition lead to a fool's paradise; and yet without intellectuality, culture and refinement a student cannot attain nor master the Secret Doctrine. Truth is not simple, except to one who knows everything. The more we know the more we confess how little we know. How silly to think that truth can be known in one short life? What Sir Isaac Newton said is true of all learned men, "I seem to have picked up but a few shells along the seashore—the great ocean of truth still lies infinite before me." So, as we overcome human nature on the physical plane, having learned the folly or evil of self indulgence, by self mastery and the enlightenment of our senses, we pass from the outer court (earth plane) of the Gentiles and the uninitiated, to the inner court of those who have learned their first lessons. Here the mental (water) and psychic (air) planes engage our earnest and patient attention.

Some study the connection, relation and correspondence between the psychical and mental planes a long time, before they realize that in order to make supernormalism a beneficent power, each supernormal faculty as well as the will must be consciously under the control of ones divinity.

To indulge supernormalism for itself alone is as dangerous and reactionary as to induldge one's senses.

Obsessions must yield to self possession, outward attractions to one's personal choice of divine freedom, sovereignty, and no one can be a master, who allows self interest, curiosity or self indulgence to control his thought or action.

The impersonal enjoyment of the spiritual life will guard and protect one from the blind alleys and temptations which lead to darkness and misery. Among those who have been delegated the called, few are "chosen" to become the disciples, to say naught of becoming the perpetual high priests after the Order of Melchizedek. If the soul must be born of water (mind), and fire (spirit), the physical man (generation-vitality) becomes transmuted into the divine man (regeneration-life). The active physical now passive becomes the passive spiritual, so that the physical is transformed by the spiritual now active.

This is the Secret Doctrine of the Bible concerning the spiritual birth, which Nicodemus as a materialist, could not grasp. John, the beloved disciple, understood, because in his gospel, he taught the Secret Doctrine, announcing the same to the initiates, in the very

first chapter. It is the logos, which
when received from the Illuminate,
qualified one to be of the Order of Melchizedek.

LECTURE IV

The Christ Psychology and Christian Mysticism.

It may here be asked, what was and is the purpose of the Secret Doctrine, which endured through the ages, perpetuated by prophets and is communicated to us in the silence* and by the spiritual Order of Melchizedek? The Holy Spirit, indefinable to vulgar intelligences, is an ever present spirit of truth, indwelling in all spiritually minded and illuminated souls by which

* Pythagoras it is said, enjoined six years of silence on his disciples. To be a mystic one must learn how to seal eyes, ears and lips to what is seen, heard and spoken. When such silence is attained, one learns how to commune with God.

truth is revealed concerning spiritual realities. The august presence of God could not approach nearer to us than does the Holy Spirit of truth.

There is however a divine technique which is concealed and revealed in the Bible, called the Christ psychology, which Jesus taught in the parables of the Five Talents and the Five Wise Virgins, and which Paul hinted at in Corinthians 11: 15. Obscure and veiled as their textual meanings are, the Secret Doctrine expounds their hidden meaning in unmistakable clearness.

Divinity, central in the soul, can illuminate the mind and life, enlighten the senses, add a divine range to sight and hearing and so permeate the soul, with its radiant and pure light as to transform ecce homo (Lo, the human!) at once into ecce deus (Lo, the God!) This is to be accepted, not only theoretically, but can be spiritually demonstrated. Biblical and secular credentials can be cited in proof of this.

Religions, among all the nations of the world articulate one central fact that life is essentially spirit and divine. It is not born of matter although associated with it. It is eternal, and therefore, the soul is immortal. This is the ever recurring theme of pure Christianity, "I am the resurrection and the life."

To prove one's Divinity and make it a conscious, helpful principle of one's life, is the supreme end of religion. All of its prophets declared this message. The martyrs died for it. And yet to day a false metaphysics and theology, advocated in part by the Christian church, has made the spiritual fact of the survival of the personality after death and the innate potential divinity of the soul a gift of God to the few, a miracle of salvation, and not the greater fact of universal, human, divine life which death cannot affect nor destroy.

In Metaphysics and Christian Science "God has been hitched to business," as though any kind of ill begotten prosperity is of His will and Providence. And yet it is a well known fact that Jesus chose to be poor (in worldly goods), that he might devote his entire time to divine service and that he might be rich in Godliness and toward God; in short, that he might not be influenced or obsessed by riches as might follow, if worldly ambition or attachment controlled him. Any sophist that makes God, who is no respector of persons, favor one class whom he blesses with wealth, and disfavor another class whom he curses with poverty, has an effete, tribal conception of God. Money, prosperity, wealth and their opposites, are largely matters of our desires, labor and ingenuity and the scriptural justification of the prosperity of the righteous is in the fact that they employ righteous, business methods to obtain, accumulate and spent riches. The rich are not rich or prosperous because only of their righteousness, nor the poor poor because only of their wickedness, but because the business of acquiring wealth even as a gift, demands of us certain social and economic qualities, which if we obey or disobey produce certain results. This is endorsed by Jesus who gave a luminous exposition of it in the parable of the five talents, when he emphasized the law of thrift and work in the accumulation of money, five talents employed bringing five more, and actually condemned the man who hid his one talent in a napkin in the earth and as a result of his indolence and stupidity, he had even that one taken from him. No one denies that justice, kindness, fair dealing, right thinking are a part of the business of becoming prosperous, but one may be all this, and if trusting only in God and seldom or never working to be prosperous, expecting prosperity to come miraculously as a result of his trust, he will remain where he is the rest of his natural life.

Not a few imagine that righteousness is a sort of hocus pocus or magic by which one is favored and blessed and another dishonored and afflicted. As it is with a seed before and after it is put into the good soil, so is it with our ideals, desires, thoughts. God helps us through conditions. He helps those who help themselves. And no sophistry is more heretical of truth, more insidious and deadly in our lives than the assumption that God is a respector of persons and not a respector of the Divine Law, that He can and does favor one class who disobey the law in practice and disfavors another class who obey it in theory only.

Mere affirmations, vain repetitions, ecstatic phrasing of texts, which are not put into practise, count for nothing.

The Secret Doctrine first of all establishes the reign of Law on all planes of life and our attainments and obtainments result from strict compliance with spiritual and scientific conditions,* established by the Law. Indeed such is the relationship between causes and effects and their resultant causes and effects, that the Law of Justice is not mocked, each soul reaping whatever it sows, not in the sense of rewards or punishments, but only in the deeper sense of spiritual and natural consequences.

The Christ psychology begins with the divine and ends with the human order of will, intelligence, feeling and life. God's will is expressed in the universe as Law,—not caprice, order—not

---

* Cor. 2: 14. ''The natural man receiveth not the things which are of the spirit of God, for they are foolishness to him; neither can he know them, for they are spiritually discerned.''

chaos; intelligence—not chance or accidents; love—not hate; life—not death. And the use we make of our willing, thinking and feeling as each one wills, thinks and feels, is registered in the character of his life. Thus the Law not only governs and finds its supreme justification in one's divinity, whence it originates, but in humanity, not only in the spiritual, but the natural world. For our divinity is in our humanity and the character of humanity is a negative or positive result of the expression of our divinity. It is the same Law governing the divine and natural man in the spiritual and natural world. The Christ psychology which differs in name only from the New Psychology hypothecates

Divinity as the fundamental key to the solution of the problems of man's life. It builds its technique on spiritual facts and knowledge. It proves its propositions by supersensuous or spiritual evidences.

These evidences to the natural man, who has not yet been enlightened or initiated into spiritual mysteries, are foolishness. But facts are stubborn things and persist until properly tabulated in the category of spiritual realities.

The mystical and scientific connection between humanity and Divinity is established by the New and Christ* psychology.

---

* Christ is the word employed to express psychological facts and processes which prove the soul to be potentially immortal and divine.

Supernormalism defines the scientific, psychic operations, faculties and results, when one functions on the subjective or spiritual side of his nature; but only when such functioning is dedicated to divine and unselfish ends can it be qualified as the application of the philosophy of the Christ psychology. Supernormal psychology is fully and exhaustively explained in the work by the author on **"The New Psychology"** and one should study and master it, to get an intelligent conception of the scope of this branch of the Christ psychology as it explains spiritual facts, which transcend the power of the normal senses and faculties to apprehend or explain. While these facts can be detached from physical causes and laws, they are none the less associated with them by causes which govern and interpenetrate them, as the ether and fourth dimension interpenetrate matter and its three dimensions in time and space. What is needed by the soul is the mystical vision, which centralized within the soul, where the spirit of God and our spirit become, as it were, fused into one and the same life and consciousness, reveals the unmistakable difference between the objective power and life of man and the same power and life when governed by and proceding from his divinity.

The Secret Doctrine affords a near vision and realization of the essential self, one's divinity, mystically uniting the soul to God, the supreme and Absolute Intelligence, where what is lawfully fixed (as matter) in time and space, but lawfully free in spirit, can be transformed and made to manifest the higher, more sublime uses of the divine will and power, co-ordinating with the lower, mental faculties and powers, to reveal the occult and divine ends, which the physical and chemical laws of matter subserve. This explains how the alleged miracles and supernaturalism of the Bible are not suspensions of natural law, nor violations of Divine principles, but the clear and undeniable evidences of law, under the soul's own divine sovereignty.

Such mystical communion between one's higher self* or Divinity and God, concerns the ego or self in the divine life, in the super consciousness, rather than in one's use of supernormal powers on the normal or supernormal plane. Mystical experiences must be and are universal and unique. Many have enjoyed them, especially prophets, mystics, philosophers, poets, avatars, great teachers. These experiences are called religious because they concern the divine life and God, but they should never be confused with merely supernormal

* Ego is the personal "1." Divinity is the Divine 1 or self universal as an entity individualized and potential in all souls. The personality is the ego objectified in the natural man or subjectified in the spiritual man. The personal ego depends upon the Divine 1 for its existence.

experiences; for while they are most useful and inevitable in the attainment of spiritual realizations, they are not directly and integrally of the impersonal spirit or the God consciousness. Such experiences are individual, and concrete, inasmuch as they relate both to Divine Guidance and human needs, but they are distinctly mystical as was the vision of the Christ to Paul while he was on the road to Damascus. Singular as such experiences are, they are of the universal Spirit, and whether in form of vision or voice, they enter the soul only when the soul is either ecstatically in communion with God, or as in the case of Paul, when the time has come for the soul to end its futile search after truth, and so to react its life from the standpoint of divine conviction and mental illumination as to enter joyfully, freely into the larger, Messianic and apostolic service. The meteor as well as the sun roll on orbits concentric with the ellipse, where the light and darkness part company forever. He who would find himself must move toward the center where God is and where the two wills, human and divine, unite and fuse at last into one.

It is supremely important that if one is of the Order of Melchizedek that he think, love and work in the outer court of the Gentiles as he serves in the Holy of Holies. One light, that of Divinity burns in singular purity in what ever he does and wherever he is!

It is not astonishing, therefore, that the word mystery and mysticism should be derived from the same root. He who incredulously and blindly permits the ego to function on only the sensuous, objective plane of consciousness, ignorantly inhibiting the soul's interior, larger and deeper expression of life and power in the sphere of its supersensuous, transcendant, subjective and subliminal consciousness, of course, will deny the reality of spiritual and mystical experiences; but, the moment the ego is disenthralled from the senses and liberated from the self imposed obsessions of its desires, and these very desires are destroyed, then the ego is free as was Paul to enjoy consciously the reveries, ecstacies, visions, voices of his soul, of angels and ministering spirits, as sent of God and as a part of the order of his divinity and destiny.

To seal the lips, close the eyes, and ears, is the first condition in concentration, which concerns the center of being and Divinity, and not any one particular subject or object of consciousness and life. Such centralization of thought, first, and then of the ego, releases the soul from bondage to sense attachments, mental habits of reaction and nervo-psychic automatisms and fortifies it against similar, sensuous temptations. A divine feeling (divine love) and thinking (truth) and being (God) transforms the nature of the soul and so, by its divinity, it is in the earth but not of it, it is living the normal life as master, under the Christ principle, and not as the obsessed, controlled slave of the carnal mind and life. To this end the Christ psychology leads and as it leads the soul, the mystic union between man and God is established.

LECTURE V

The Key—How Applied. Divine Realization and Illumination.

Mysticism leads to divine realization and illumination. Its supreme purpose is to clear the consciousness of all veils, shadows, mists, obsessions, inhibitions, habits, prejudices, objective and subjective obstructions which deflect, but do not reflect Divinity. A realization of one's own Divinity is tantamount to the attainment of God consciousness, which is known and defined by eastern mystics as the super consciousness, because it is paramount to all other forms of it.

The Secret Doctrine would not be either secret or sacred were it to divulge knowledge which could avail the charlatan or the magician. Therein lie its safeguard and peculiarity. The knowledge it reveals is supernormalism plus mysticism. A free use of supernormal powers employed for personal or selfish purposes is possible and practical, but it leads to the blind alleys of spiritual occultation. Such use of our powers is discouraged, if for no other reason than that it frequently leads to dementia. Persons, not students, who defy scientific and divine warnings of seers, psychological experts and teachers of mysticism, and refuse to obey conditions, ''rushing in where angels fear to tread," have no one to blame but themselves for the disasters which overtake them. The Secret Doctrine is exact and severe in demanding the spiritual life as of paramount importance among students of occult science, experimenters, demonstrators. This life is impersonal, universal, cosmic, and the foundation on which is built the conscious perception of spiritual revelation, divine realization and illumination.

Supernormalism is not mediumship. It affirms self-possession, freedom and conscious sovereignty against obsession, control and unconscious dependency. The phrase spiritual gifts, employed by Paul (Corinthians 14) refers to supernormalism, not mediumship or supernaturalism. Supernaturalism as used by theologians implies an accidental or sporadic happening impossible under natural and spiritual law, traceable to an alleged fiat of God, to whom spontaneity of action is a privilege inexplicable to human reason, even in the absolute perfection of the Divine Will. Evolution, in a divine sense, implies involution, but does not deny the innate, potential, ultimate perfection of the soul. Creation suggests recreation, as generation, regeneration and death, the resurrection. Supernormalism signifies no accidental fiat of God, because His eternal plan failed or because the soul from birth in matter could and would not save itself from ignorance, weakness, sin and sickness as does the word supernaturalism, but affirms the enfolded, involved potentialities of divine being, which, when expressed, prove one's divinity and mystically associates man with God. This is important to perceive, for when it is understood, one can understand the difference between mediumship which is largely an organic and psychic peculiarity of human nature, than a spiritual attainment, as is illustrated by the comparative meanings of the words medium and adopt, or magician and necromancer, sorcerer and hierophant, prophet and Christ. There can be no mistake in either scientific or spiritual definitions.

The impersonal, divine use of powers, whether normal or supernormal, makes the degree of difference between the one set of words and the other, which the word, supernaturalism does not convey except to make confusion more confounded.

Supernaturalism implies miracle, while supernormalism implies mystery, which science can explain. To see, hear, feel spiritually, so that one can function on the astral plane, see visions, hear voices, commune with spiritual beings in the spiritual world, telepath, receive inspirations and revelations consciously, prophesy, heal, interpret visions, know the deep things of God,—to do these things may be mysterious, but not

miraculous, which a knowledge of supernormalism will readily explain. So that it is ignorance which makes supernormal attainments seem miracles, but it is knowledge which dissolves the mystery.

The connecting link between man and God, morals and revelation, the lost key, the stone which the builders rejected, metaphysically conceived, the psychology which was the lost word and discovered cabalistically mixed with chimera, fantasy, parables, myths, symbols, conceits of all kinds, is supernormalism, which furnishes the true foundation on which mysticism or divine realization are founded. This the Secret Doctrine of the Bible recovers and restates in intelligible language, so that no one need grope any more in darkness or ignorance.*

Melchizedek, so long mysteriously and remotely connected with man's earliest life, thought and destiny, is no longer to be esteemed an historical man without birth and lineage, but Divinity, personated as the Holy Spirit or the Spirit of Truth, which is indwelling within every human soul, and preparing humanity for its highest orders, to be a perpetual priest at the divine altar,

---

* For full and detailed instruction, study the "System of Philosophy Concerning Divinity," mail course of fifty-six lessons, five series of teachings. Read also books on "The Philosophy Concerning the Divinity of Clairvoyance," cloth $1.50, and "The Philosophy Concerning the Divinity of Clairaudience," paper, 75 cents, by the author.

where, as in the Holy of Holies, the pure white spirit burns with an ineffable and inextinguishable glory. The lamp may become useless, the oil be burnt up, the wick die down to a mere bit of carbon, but the soul with its radiant, eternal light will shine on and on forever.

Supernormal psychology is a lamp to man's feet. It orders his mind to a cosmic scheme, and keys his heart to a celestial vibration. It reveals his eternality and infinity in his Divinity. It explains the reason of Law and the Law of reason. It proves the Bible to be as the fig tree, concealing the fruit under the shadow of its literature, or as the cocoanut, containing the water of life within its historical shell.

It shows that Adam and Eve, were not the first father and mother of the human race, but the electro magnetic type of the active and passive principle of the universe, in which, as in the human organism, the soul short circuits God, to find that he can cut himself temporarily from his supply and Divinity, only to be forced by the negative and positive law of his being, (action and reaction) to find life and immortality, unity and oneness in the very God, in whom he ignorantly lives, moves and has his being. This is the science of eternal life. Mere existence, is nothing. Divine realization is everything. The conscious knowledge that in the sovereign power of Divine love, the soul discovers God, as in the passion of human love, it loses God, is the sublime and perpetual revelation of religion, which occult physiology explains as the maculate and immaculate conception of the incarnation of God, in the human race, and which occult psychology reveals as the inhibition and exhibition of the super consciousness, the Christ life, wherein our own Divinity denies or bears witness to God.

Man in the microcosm and God in the macrocosm are of one divine Being. The soul's triumph over the flesh and carnal mind demonstrates its celestial origin and destiny. Melchizedek, without birth or death, family or genealogy, clothing, Abraham (historical man) with the mantle of his majestic and sovereign Divinity, typifies that our Divinity—the Divinity of man, thus sheltered and protected through the ages,—like the lily in the mud, will rise to express the Christ, and affirm, "I am the Resurrection and the Life."

DIVINE SCIENCE AND ITS BRANCHES WITH TECHNIQUE OR PRACTICAL DEMONSTRABLE METHODS

Your Need Supplied.

COURSE 1.

Divine Science of Healing.

Jesus is not on earth now to tell the sick, worried, hopeless, miserable how to be well, happy and strong. His teaching, however, is here, and a few are gifted with divine inspiration and practical divine knowledge in the science of healing which he taught to reveal the secret of the doctrine to others. It can be learned. The patient can put its technique into practice and resurrect himself by his own Divine Will, Power and Life. "Those that are whole need no physician." True, but those that are sick need a metaphysician.

Method of Technique.

So called miracles of Healing wrought thousands of years ago are possible today. Dr. Grumbine presents the science in a simple, lucid, luminous, practical way, within the reach of all. Truth is like a key. It opens all doors of possibility if you possess the key. Dr. Grumbine presents you the key. Have you studied his course? Your education is not complete without it. This is admitted by all who know.

For the benefit of the New Thoughter. Who is Dr. Grumbine?

He was a pioneer New Thoughter, before there were any National or Local Centers. He is a Metaphysician, a Teacher of Divine Science, The New Psychology and Christian Mysticism, and has been before the public since 1888, with nearly thirty years on the New Thought platform. Among his students who afterwards became teachers and practitioners are Kate Atkinson Boehme, author, Dr. Julia Seton, Lucy C. McGee, Boston, Mrs. Mary C. Chapin, New York City, and many others. The press is unanimous in his praise.

Read these Statements.

"*The Fellowship Messenger,*" Omaha, Nebraska, writes: "For a year and a half past I have promoted a great many Metaphysical lectures, but there has been nothing equal in soundness and catholicity of its teaching to that which Dr. Grumbine in promulgating."

Kate Atkinson Boehme, New Thought Author and Healer, wrote: "Such richness of thought, diversity of expression and originality of conception are rarely combined in one individual."

"*The Harbinger of Light,*" Melbourne, Australia, wrote: "As a teacher it is questionable if his superior, for the past thirty years at least, has been on the platform."

"*Lillian Whiting,*" author "The World Beautiful," etc., wrote: "Your work is marvelous—epoch making."

The Course by Mail.

A course of twelve lessons, with technique is offered the earnest, sincere student who seeks for freedom or longs to be a practitioner and to demonstrate. There can be no better, more luminous course by any one. Each lesson is brief, concise and a revelation. No superfluous language to camouflage the truth. The light shines with clear beauty through each word and thought.

The cost is but ten dollars for this special course.

Special.

Dr. Grumbine prepares students for the New Thought and Divine Science platform. Such students should study his complete system to finish their New Thought or Divine Science education. Eventually you will take his system. Why not now?

Special courses on

Course II.   (Sixth Sense)
         "Clairsentience," 12 Lessons.

Course III.   "Inspiration," 12 lessons.

Course IV. "Illumination," 10 lessons.

Each may be taken separately.

Fee for each course, **$10.00**.

Address:

J. C. F. GRUMBINE

1916 East 105th St., Cleveland, Ohio.

THE SYSTEM OF PHILOSOPHY CONCERNING DIVINITY.

Mail Course.

Correspondence School, Established 1894, by J. C. F. Grumbine, B. D., Fellow of the Society of Science, Letters and Arts, London, England, Noted Author, World Traveller and Member of the National Geographical Society. A Teacher of Divine Science, the Spiritual Philosophy, Including Theosophy and the New Psychology.

It is known to all the world, that Divine Science, affirming the reality of Spirit and Divinity of the soul, is true, admitted to be so by the most eminent scientists—Sir Oliver Lodge, Camille

Flammarion, Sir William Crookes, the late Dr. Frederick Meyer, Signor Lombroso, Dr. Hodgson and Professor James and numerous other leaders in chemistry, psychology, physics, literature and the church.

Our duty now is to express our supernormal powers, in a sane, conscious, scientific manner and to realize our Divinity.

Our supernormal or psychical powers can be arranged into two distinct classes. By powers we mean our ability or capacity to express our divinity, hold communion with the spiritual world, function on the supernormal planes, to heal, to telepath, to learn one's vocation in life, so as to be successful, prosperous, and well and to obtain intromission to celestial knowledge and revelations, to exercise all the divine powers which hitherto have been regarded as impossible, and supernatural.

Mr. Grumbine specializes on supernormal psychology. He cannot emphasize too strongly the fact that all possess supernormal powers, and should express them. It is divine to do so and a help to the higher life.

Supernormal powers are natural. We are conscious, free, independent, when we become supernormal. The supernormal powers are spiritual seeing, hearing, feeling, seership, prevision, psychometry, intuition, realization, illumination, healing, ecstasy, telepathy, divine inspiration, projection of the double, functioning on the astral plane, consciously. These we all can express—some to a greater degree than others, because they will spend more time and be more earnest in their efforts.

What is claimed can be done for all is being done for each student by Grumbine's System, and your testimony will be added when you study the profound but simple System which he teaches.

Take Theosophy; Dr. Grumbine affords the initiated or inner circle a very esoteric and practical teaching. There is nothing sectarian about the teaching. Your freedom is never curtailed. He has received word from those who have taken this work that the System taught by mail through "**The College of Divine Sciences and Realization,**" the correspondence school, is superior in many ways to any other esoteric teaching. The language is less stuffed with Orientalisms, while his methods are scientific and adapted to the simplest minds. One physician, a student who took the System years ago, wrote that it is the System par excellence.

His teachings are pure divine Science, presented in a way to appeal to the most enlightened as well as the uninformed.

He is positively opposed to fortune

telling and commercialism in New Thought. In his System the way is shown to the highest service, practically and spiritually.

To commune or communicate consciously with our invisible, divine helpers, even the Holy Spirit, is possible for each one, and it is far and away the best method and brings the most reliable, beneficent and happiest results. But— and mark the condition—one cannot expect to succeed in becoming an adept, unless he lives the spiritual life.

J. C. F. Grumbine is an expert in these branches of Divine Science and the New Psychology, and is famed the world over as a superior, conscientious and reliable teacher. The knowledge he gives is a revelation in itself. He has been before the public since 1893.

Divine Science Versus Christian Science.

Divine Science as taught by the System, is the foundation of Christian Science and is a science older than the Bible and is not glorifying or dependent upon the personality of a man or a woman. Without Divine Science there could be no Christian Science. The **"System of Philosophy Concerning Divinity"** reveals the technique of Divine Healing (for which we are informed by Christian Scientists themselves, Christian Science charges $100), in a language so clear and simple and demonstrations so practical and irresistible, that any intelligent person can grasp them.

The Order of the White Rose

A School with a Destiny—An Order which is Rosicrucian—Founded in 1894.

The Series or System by Mail.

The five series of revealed teachings comprehending the System apply to human needs, because man is essentially divine. If spiritual unfoldment or divine realization is not possible under the direction of this System, then there is little hope for the human race. Preparation to perceive and receive the truth is from within. By a psychological process and psychological formulae,

99

evidences and demonstrations are accomplished.

Each one who seeks expression of supernormal powers and the realization of one's divinity, can have it, because each one is divine.

Mysticism and Rosicrucianism.

The Hermetic Law, Theosophy, Biblical Mysteries, the Vedanta Philosophy, and Rosicrucianism are fully explained in the System.

Psychism.

Your hidden psychical powers are made manifest sanely by this System, if rules are applied. Obsessions, control, trances, unconsciousness, are discountenanced. The System affirms personal sovereignty, self-mastery, con-ciousness, freedom in the highest sense.

Normal Course.

A normal course follows the System. This course furnishes the key to the hidden wisdom of the Bible, also to all symbols, myths, allegories, numbers, the cabala and occult psychology.

Words of Praise.

"Dr. Grumbine drew from all who had the pleasure of hearing him, noth-ing but admiration and praises. As teacher and lecturer he is par-excel-lence. Scholarly, philosophic, profound, eloquent, inspirational, yet withal lucid and easy to follow, both on the platform and in class work, he is one of the most impressive teachers yet to come before

the Omaha New Thought Fellowship.
From the 1st to the 12th of January, a
course of New Thought Lectures was
given in the Fellowship audience room,
by Dr. J. C. F. Grumbine of Boston.

"As an instructor of the New
Thought, Dr. Grumbine is very patient,
there being nothing cheap or frivolous
in his methods. He has a message for
the world and he feels it his duty (pro-
vided that is the appropriate word to
use), to proclaim it in all sincerity. His
ideals are of the spiritual type: his philosophy is cosmic in cast and impersonal
in spirit. As a New Thoughtist, he gives
the student the advantage of all good
things to be found in every branch of
learning; as a student and teacher of

the 'New Psychology' he unfolds the mystery of being on the three planes of matter, mind and spirit, in such terms and with such wealth of thought and research as to make his lectures veritable treasuries of physical, occult and spiritual knowledge. He has sounded the depths and ascended the heights in that kingdom where the streets of life may be found, and beheld therein glories of the seen and unseen world, and so found a place where the illuminati, whose wisdom is of inestimable value to less unfolded souls in their search for truth, the divine light of knowledge, and the laws of self-unfoldment.

"In coming to Omaha, Dr. Grumbine made many friends and awakened some minds to a deeper and sweeter perception of the spiritual worth of each life, and lifted the veil for some eyes to behold the divine radiance of the soul immortal."—The Fellowship Messenger.

This interesting personal item from Mr. John H. Davis, of Columbus, Ohio, will be inspiring to new students. "I want to take this opportunity to thank you for the immense amount of benefit that I have received from personal contact with you, and hearing your instructive lectures which have aided me wonderfully in spiritual unfoldment, which in turn has given me a broader outlook on life and a more complete understanding of my true relationship to God and man, more wisdom and a much happier life."

Mr. Grumbine often travels on lecture engagements. Indulge delays. Your letter will receive attention as soon as it reaches him.

The System of Philosophy Concerning Divinity.

TERMS.

What are you doing to express or realize your Divinity?

You are one of a large class who do not realize that you can develop supernormal powers and become master of the circumstances of your life. You can! We all possess supernormal faculties and should express them. We are better off if we do. But where will this class go, or turn for help? I add—to this System; first, because it is the only System of its kind that can help you, and secondly because **The System as a Mail Course, with 56 Lessons, covers all the Conditions and Rules governing the Law, expression of Supernormalism.**

The lack in most Christian New Thoughtists, Divine Scientists, is a knowledge of Supernormal Psychology and Mystic Science of the Bible which eliminates such words as supernaturalism, miracle and magic from their vocabulary, and enables them by Dr. Grumbine's system to positively know and demonstrate.

The High School and University graduate, the Character Analyst, the

Psycho-Therapist, the mother or father who plans big things for their boys and girls, who, without a knowledge of their vocational adaptation in business or life, as well as the more spiritually minded, can find in the system the illumination they need to fit them for their life work.

THE FEE.

(Reduced from $60.)

For $25.00 cash or $35.00 in $5.00 monthly payments($10.00 the first payment), you can study, not buy the System.

Students entered any time.

Fee includes two text books.

Send P. O. or Express Money Order

(please do not send personal check, un-less you allow extra for discount) to J. C. F. Grumbine, 1916 East 105th St., Cleveland, Ohio.

J. C. F. GRUMBINE'S BOOKS

The Order of the White Rose Publications.

The Noted Author, New Thought and Divine Science Lecturer and World Traveler. Life Member of the Society of Science, Literature and Art, London, England, and Member of the National Geographical Society.

THE NEW PSYCHOLOGY.

"Melchizedek or the Secret Doctrine of the Bible." Never before have the mysteries been made so clear. A wonderful revelation. Cloth, $1.50.

"New Thought for Children" (in press,) cloth.

The don'ts, can'ts and mustn'ts connected by affirmative teaching. Price $1.00.

"Psychometry, or, The Sixth Sense," the science of kinesthesia, fourth edition, is a simple but profound exposition of this most fascinating subject, put before the reader in the language which is both clear and dignified and which opens the eyes to the inner spheres of the soul and the law for the expression of this soul-power called sensitiveness or soul-measurement. Any one with this book can unfold this psychometric power. Price, 50 cts.

"Auras and *Colors,"* fourth edition, is a very instructive book and inasmuch as it is now in its eighth thousand, proves its value as an original contribution on this very occult subject. How to see the aura, how to know the significance of the colors one vibrates, how to place them, how to

catalogue all colors correctly, what colors to wear, healing power of color, are here briefly and concisely explained. Price, 75 cts.

"*Concentration*" (in press). The key. A masterful work. Board covers. Price, $1.00.

"*Beckoning Hands From the Near Beyond,*" cloth. The book of the hour for those who mourn or seek scientific knowledge of the Beyond. Price, $1.50.

"*Boston Lectures on The New Psychology,*" cloth. The book which reveals the deep mysteries of the soul. Price, $1.50.

"*Telepathy,*" fourth edition. A new book which proves the origin of thought; how God inspires us, how we telepath thoughts to each other. It explains the telepathic code, or how to transfer thoughts. It shows that Divinity explains telepathy, and not telepathy Divinity. Cloth, $1.50. Paper, 75 cts.

"*The Psychology of color.*" Cloth. A wonderfully fascinating study now made most popular by scientific discoveries. Price, $1.50.

STANDARD BOOKS ON OCCULT AND DIVINE SCIENCE.

"*Clairvoyance, or The Spiritual Perception.*" Fifth edition. Since the publication of Emanuel Swedenborg's books, no more helpful, valuable work has appeared than the one entitled "Clairvoyance: Its Nature and Laws of Unfoldment." It is a revelation concerning the Divinity of perception and seeing, how to unfold the spiritual vision, to pierce the veil of sense, enter at will into the spiritual world, and become a seer and an adept in this branch of mystical science. This is the first book ever published on this subject. Price, cloth $1.50.'

"Your work is marvelous—epoch making."—*Lillian Whiting.*

"The lessons which constitute the volume are of great use to all who desire to familiarize themselves with both the clearest scientific view of Clairvoyance yet presented to the reading public, and the most efficacious means of developing the faculty in themselves by means of simple and very practical experiments, which many of Mr. Grumbine's students in various places have found highly beneficial in many ways. All sincere students of the psychic realm will do well to read and study this excellent volume."—*W. J. Colville, noted author.*

"*Clairaudience,*" the only scientific text book of its kind that teaches students how to express their own supernormal power of concentration and hearing and so to realize spiritual communion, solve the problems of the Voice and the Voices. Paper, 75 cts.

"*Easy Lessons in Occult Science,*" fourth edition, is a neat book containing much very helpful knowledge not found elsewhere, on how to proceed to unfold the independent psychical powers without going into a trance or becoming obsessed. It is a text book for beginners who contemplate making the most of themselves, both in a human and a divine sense, and who realize that failure in the world is mostly due to not knowing how to lay hold of all one's powers which lie dormant within us. Price, paper 50 cts.

"*The Great Secret and Other Occult Tales,*" is a series of short stories on occult science. Price, paper 75 cts.

"*The Spirit World—What and Where It Is.*" This is a most valuable contribution to this won-

114

derfully great subject. Every line in the book is scientific and dependable. It is just the work for those who are bereaved. Each topic handled exhaustively. Subjects treated in a concise and convincing manner are: *"Death", "Life", "The Location and Geography of The Spirit World", "Destiny", "Messages From the Spirit World", and "Conditions and Means of Spirit Communications".* Price, 50 cts.

To agents who sell New Thought and Occult literature 25% is allowed on five or more listed copies, postage prepaid to any address. No books sent out on approval or commission. All orders must be accompanied with cash.

Address, *J. C. F. GRUMBINE,*

1916 East 105th St., Cleveland, Ohio.

(Unless otherwise directed.)

WHAT IS NEW THOUGHT AND WHO IS THE NEW THOUGHTER?

What is new Thought?

1. It teaches that God is Spirit, within each one, omnipresent, omniscient, omnipotent, expressed in all consciousness and life as unchanging law, in both the natural and spiritual world. Our own Divinity should be sovereign.

2. It teaches that pure and universal religion is impersonal and is the science of truth, of God demonstrable through one's own Divinity.

3. It teaches that all Bibles, contain revelations of truth, but are not infallible as historical or doctrinal books.

4. It teaches that the Christ spirit wherever expressed, is the highest, purest, most perfect realization and metaphysical concept of the working principle of Divine love and life in mankind.

5. It teaches that disease, failure, poverty are not the result of God's wrath and punishment, but of man's ignorance and the limitations placed on his human and divine potentialities and prerogatives; and it affirms that when mankind lives the Christ life on earth, (the golden rule for service) and thinks and acts righteously,—poverty, disease and failure will pass away. This refers to economic, political and spiritual conditions.

6. It teaches a demonstrable immor-

tality and conscious communion of spirit. This is New Thought in a nutshell.

Who is the New Thoughter?

A New Thoughter is one who accepts the above, lives it in his life and supports it by his presence and money.

There are many groups of so-called New Thoughters who place special emphasis on one, two or more of the six propositions.

Group One.

The first group is the highest in spiritual service and life who are absolutely living up to the five propostions. They subordinate their **personal** and **selfish** interests to the good of the common movement and seek to live in the

Universal Spirit. They are trying to unite and fuse all centers into one homogeneous and harmonious body of kindred hearts whose ideal is set on divine unity and unselfish human fellowship and service. They do not wish to profit by the movement, to pose as speakers, healers and managers, but so to live and prepare themselves for the New Thought and Divine Science Ideal and Vision on earth as to be worthy to be called and chosen to serve whenever the voice of God calls them, and put under foot their own personal claims or wishes to be a leader or a mouthpiece of God! Such are the true disciples and workers. These have not neglected to prepare themselves, so far as the demands

of the platform and field are concerned
with the necessary education to make
the ideal and the message they present
acceptable.

Group Two.

Under group two must be classified
all "babes in truth," who use any given
or established New Thought or Divine
Science organization to know the law
of freedom and truth, so that they can
be of service to mankind. They may be
attached or unattached to an orthodox
church but who, unless wisely guided
are sometimes misled to modify and
tincture New Thought Philosophy with
special confusing theories which they
had once entertained and accepted when
in the Christian Church, and which now.

are so deeply imbedded in their subconscious minds that the word "freedom" is easily translated into the word "bondage," in which their **peculiar views, personal opinions and idiosyncracies** as to what New Thought should be are predominant. Instead of **accepting truth for authority, they unconsciously or consciously accept authority for truth.** Unless these "babes in truth" can be fully enlightened and made to surrender these false and personal theories for the Universal Divine Spirit and God consciousness, they will sooner or later strike the danger reefs of sectarianism and dogmatism which lurk in the shallow waters of personal views and experiences.

Group Three.

This group includes the self lovers and seekers who call themselves "New Thoughters" and yet fail to hold up their hands to be counted or to give their money to support the movement. They, perhaps, buy a book or two on New Thought, subscribe for a popular New Thought periodical, attend a New Thought meeting when a new teacher or healer enters a city, but never identify themselves or cooperate with any organized center. They are the "newspaper New Thoughters", who "want what they want when they want it".

Group Four.

Then there is the last group, which furnish the spurs, inspirations and literature of New Thought and Divine Science Movement, whose teachers teach freedom of thought in all departments of knowledge, and are representative pioneers of that liberalism which limits no one and yet does not attempt to confine truth to any one "personal" idea, viewpoint, center, Bible, interpretation or experience, but includes in their thought and love all who differ with them. These teachers see good and affirm the truth in all religions, philosophies, science and do not narrow the truth to what some, in their ignorance and prejudices, maintain to be all there is of truth, because they think it.

A Final Word.

Success comes to those who know and apply the law. Truth will triumph over all adversaries. Each one must learn by dear bought experience the difference between "human" opinions and "divine" truth, between "human" leading and "divine" guidance. It will take time to educate the ignorant and inexperienced in divine knowledge, but that is the work of the patient, sincere, consecrated leaders. So long as we get rid of selfishness, ignorance, envy, self-seeking and self-praise, the advance and prosperity of the movement is assured. But our duty is to be loyal to the Spirit of Truth, which commands us to sacrifice the **personal** for the **Universal** and our own selfish interests and opinions for the one Divine Center of truth and love, within each one where unity and harmony alone can obtain.